Staying Alive

Gary Miller

Published by
Sundance Publishing
33 Boston Post Road West
Suite 440
Marlborough, MA 01752
800-343-8204
www.sundancepub.com

Staying Alive
ISBN 978-0-7608-9628-0

Illustrations by Tony Gregio ,

Photo Credits
cover ©Francesc Muntada/CORBIS; p. 1 ©Joe McDonald/CORBIS; pp. 6, 7 (leaf
frog) ©Alfred Molon; p. 7 (katydid) ©Jennifer Foeller, (chameleon) ©Strauss/
Curtis/CORBIS, (sea horse) ©Ximena Jeria; p. 8 ©Kennan Ward/CORBIS; p. 9
(angelfish pattern) ©Richard Ng; p. 10 ©Kevin Schafer/CORBIS; p. 11 (brook
trout) ©Richard Gunion, (flying squirrel) ©Joe McDonald/CORBIS, (frog) ©Randy
M. Ury/CORBIS, (turtle, top) ©Stephen Frink/CORBIS, (turtle, bottom) ©Robert
Yin/CORBIS; p. 12 (deer) ©Randy M. Ury/CORBIS, (hare, left, center) ©Kennan
Ward/CORBIS, (hare, right) ©Tom Brakefield/CORBIS; p. 13 (top) ©Brandon Cole,
(bottom) ©Stephen Wong; p. 16 ©Gerold and Cynthia Merker/Visuals Unlimited;
p. 17 ©Joe McDonald/CORBIS; pp. 18–19 (butterflies) Scott Camazine/Photo
Researchers, Inc.; p. 19 ©George D. Lepp/CORBIS; p. 20 (illustration of paradise
whydah) Richard Brown, (finch) ©Warwick Tarboton/Gallo Images/CORBIS; p. 21
(birds) ©Arthur Morris/Visuals Unlimited, (nest) ©Robert Domm/Visuals
Unlimited; p. 24 (great horned owl) ©Royalty-Free/CORBIS, (eyes) ©James
Ravilious/Beaford Archive/CORBIS; p. 25 (snake, top) ©Joe McDonald/CORBIS,
(mouse) ©Naturfoto Honal/CORBIS, (snake, bottom) ©W. Perry Conway/CORBIS;
p. 26 ©William Manning/CORBIS; p. 27 (center) ©Horst Gossmann, (bottom)
©David A. Northcott/CORBIS; p. 28 ©Joe McDonald/CORBIS

Printed by Nordica International Ltd.
Manufactured in Guangzhou, China
September, 2011
Nordica Job#: CA21101435
Sundance/Newbridge PO#: 226732

Table
of Contents

Blending In

When they need to, these animals can fade out of sight. How? Their colors and patterns are the key.

The world of animals is a tough one. Survival depends on finding food—and avoiding becoming food for others. For many animals, color is a way to do both. Their colors help them stay hidden.

Nature hides some animals so well that they're almost impossible to see. Their colors, patterns, and textures may all fool you. So look closely for these animals— or you might not see them at all!

Nature's Cover-Ups

Some animals survive because they're good at staying hidden. Look at the picture below and see if you can find the frog. It might take you a while to see that it's hidden among the dry leaves on the forest floor. That's because nature has given the frog a special disguise called **camouflage**. Camouflage helps the frog blend in with its environment.

The frog's body color is the same color as the dry leaves. Its skin is bumpy like a leaf, too. And to make the frog even harder to see, its body is shaped a little bit like a leaf. To a **predator** like a snake, the frog is invisible. And that's the way this frog stays alive!

THIS FROG stays perfectly still when a predator comes near.

How good a predator would you be?

Some animals blend in so well with their environment that it's almost impossible to see them.

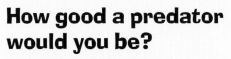

Where are those guys?

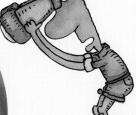

Katydid

Chameleon

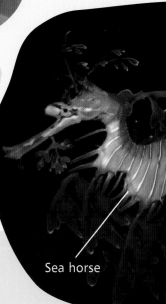

Sea horse

See me now?

Can You Spot It?

Have you ever wondered why so many animals have spots or stripes? Take the jaguar. Its spots are more than just decoration. They help the jaguar blend in with its **environment**. This helps the jaguar to stay hidden from its **prey**—the animals it hunts.

How do spots and stripes help an animal to hide? This works because some animals, like dogs and cats, can only see in a few colors. For animals with this limited vision, other animals that are all one color really stand out. So spots or stripes break up an animal's coloring, and this makes an animal harder to see—whether it is hiding or hunting.

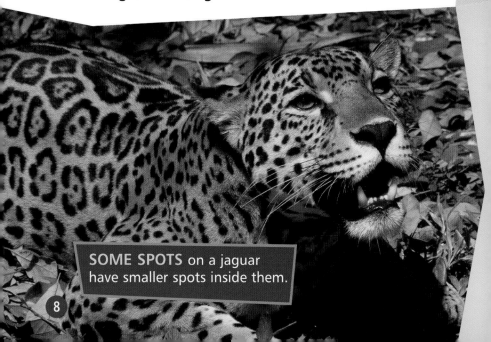

SOME SPOTS on a jaguar have smaller spots inside them.

How Patterns Help

A black-and-white comparison, like the one below, can show you how patterns help animals to blend in with their environment.

What animals do these patterns belong to?

These patterns make me dizzy.

1. Giraffe
2. Zebra
3. Angelfish
4. Barred rock chicken

Top to Bottom

Some animals live where it's very hard to stay hidden. Birds spend much of their time in the sky. Fish and frogs live in a world of water. These animals can be seen by their predators from above and below. How do these animals stay hidden? They use **countershading**. This means that their bodies are darker on top and lighter below. The Atlantic puffin is one example.

ATLANTIC PUFFINS are also called sea parrots.

Dark top

Light bottom

Everything looks so dark down there!

Animals That Have Countershading

The Atlantic puffin nests on the ocean shore and hunts for small fish. The puffin's dark-colored top helps it blend in with dark rocks or with dark ocean water. This helps to protect it from predators above it. When the bird swims, its white belly faces down. The white feathers help the bird blend in with the light sky above.

Brook trout

Flying squirrel

Frog

LOOKING DOWN at it, the sea turtle blends in with the deep, dark waters.

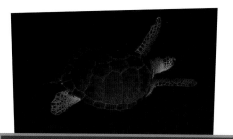

LOOKING UP at it, the turtle blends in with the light from the water's surface.

11

Color Matters

Sometimes an animal's color puts it in more danger. A whitetail deer has a brown coat. That makes it easy for the deer to hide in brush or dry leaves. But in winter, the deer's dark coat stands out against the snow. That's enough to make a hungry coyote jump for joy!

Nature helps other animals get around these problems by changing their colors. The snowshoe hare is brown in the summer. But in winter, it sheds its brown coat and grows a white one. That way, the hare can hide in snow. Sorry, coyote!

THE HARE'S COLOR changes from all brown to white, starting with the ears and feet.

Quick-Change Artist

No animal changes its looks faster or more dramatically than the cuttlefish. This relative of the octopus can change its color, color pattern, even the texture of its skin, in seconds. The skin of a cuttlefish is filled with tiny sacs of color that look like tiny dots. The cuttlefish can use its muscles to shrink the dots or make them bigger. This lets the cuttlefish change color quickly.

AN OCTOPUS can also use color to communicate. The female of one type of octopus can make the area around her beak, or mouth, bright green to attract males.

I think green's my color.

13

Great Pretenders

Nature has given some creatures a different trick to help them stay alive. They are masters of disguise.

If you have ever been to a Halloween party, you know how much fun costumes can be. Unlike people, some animals have disguises that last a lifetime.

Why do some animals look almost exactly like other animals? It isn't for fun. This gift from nature provides extra protection that helps them to survive.

Deadly Double

If you saw both of these snakes in the wild, could you tell which was which? You better look closely because it could be a matter of life and death. The bite of the coral snake below is so deadly that it can kill you. The bite of the king snake on the right is not poisonous.

Many of the snakes' predators can't tell the difference, either. This makes the king snake's life a lot easier because when a predator sees a king snake, it thinks twice before attacking. It could be a coral snake.

CORAL SNAKES are shy, so your chances of seeing one are small.

KING SNAKES are called "false coral snakes."

Reptile Rap

How can you tell the difference between the coral snake and the king snake? The arrangement of the red stripes is the key. Snake experts remember this rhyme:

**Red next to black, friend to Jack.
Red next to yellow, kill a fellow.**

Q: What do you get when a king snake bites you?
A: *A royal pain!*

17

Fooled You!

Can you tell these two butterflies apart? Most birds can't. So they avoid both of them. Why? Because one of them tastes terrible!

As a caterpillar, the monarch butterfly below eats milkweed, which has a bitter-tasting sap. And this makes the butterfly taste awful. So once a bird has eaten a monarch, it probably doesn't want to eat another one. All of this helps the viceroy butterfly on the right.

Quit copying me!

THE MONARCH has two rows of white dots on the edges of its wings.

Scientists think that over a long period of time, viceroys changed until they were almost **identical** to monarchs. This helps the viceroy stay alive because its colors and patterns send the message, "Don't eat me. I taste terrible."

Monarch caterpillar feeding on milkweed

Ugh! I'll take worms any day.

Black band

THE VICEROY has a black band on its back wings.

Fake Out!

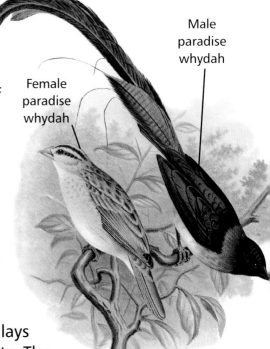

Male paradise whydah

Female paradise whydah

Caring for a baby bird takes up a lot of its mother's time. Unless you're a bird called the paradise whydah. The female whydah is a **brood parasite**. She has another bird do the work of motherhood for her!

This African trickster lays her eggs in finch nests. The finch doesn't notice because the whydah's eggs look just like finch eggs!

And if that's not enough, baby whydahs look exactly like baby finches. They even act and sound like baby finches. So the mother finch does all the work of feeding and caring for the baby whydahs. She can't tell her own babies from the whydah babies!

Finch

Match Game

Some American birds are as tricky as the whydah. One is called the brown-headed cowbird. It lays its eggs in the nests of more than 100 other types of birds. The other birds don't seem to notice!

Cowbird chicks are usually larger and grow faster than the real chicks of the mother bird.

I'm your kid. I'm just big boned.

Can you spot the cowbird egg?

Q: Why was the mother cowbird sad?
A: Because her eggs were spotted!

Super Senses

If these animals were human, they'd have senses like superheroes. Nature has given them super senses to help them stay alive.

Did you ever notice that dogs sniff everything? That's because a dog's nose is supersensitive. With one sniff of the air, a dog can tell if a friend has walked by recently. A dog can also tell if there's a tasty snack in the area, or even if one of its enemies is hiding behind a nearby tree.

Dogs aren't the only animals with super senses. Creatures from rattlesnakes to bats can hear, see, smell, and feel things in a way that humans just can't.

Sensing Supper

You may have trouble seeing in the dark. But some animals have no problem at all. The great horned owl, for example, has very large eyes. Its **pupils,** which let light into the eyes, are very large, too. Inside its eyes are many tiny parts that sense light. This helps the owl see and hunt in the dark.

Great horned owl

Night Sight

An owl's pupils are huge at night, which allows in great amounts of light. This lets owls see 35 to 100 times better than humans can in dim light.

They're the Pits

These tiny holes near the rattlesnake's eyes are its pits. Snakes with this special organ are called pit vipers.

Pit

The rattlesnake is a night hunter with special senses, too. Right near the snake's eyes are its **pits**. The pits let the snake sense the body heat of other animals. In total darkness, a rattler can feel the heat of a mouse that is up to 100 yards away. It can tell exactly where the mouse is within 2 to 6 feet and can strike it with no problem. So if you see a mouse and there's a rattler in the area, tell the mouse to stay cool!

Uh-oh. He's getting warmer....

I Smell Dinner!

Although the turkey vulture has great eyesight, to find food it usually starts with its sense of smell. This bird is commonly thought to be a **raptor,** or bird of prey. It dines mostly on animals, such as squirrels, rabbits, and deer, that are already dead. And it can smell a meal from a mile away!

The wind carries the smell of a dead animal from the ground up into the sky, and the vulture sniffs it out. Once a vulture smells a dead animal, the bird can then use its excellent vision to spot it on the ground. The bird swoops down, and it's mealtime!

THE STOMACH of a vulture can digest meat that has been dead for a long time.

Where should we go to lunch?

Well, I smell something tasty on Route 66.

Just Follow the Other Guy's Nose!

The black vulture is a raptor, too. But its sense of smell is poor. So how does it find food? Easy—it uses its eyes. The black vulture follows the turkey vulture around. When the turkey vulture finds food, the black vulture dives in and steals itself a share!

THE VULTURE USES its can-opener-shaped beak to pry open the body of its prey.

Bat Vision

You might have heard the expression "blind as a bat." But in darkness, bats do an amazing job of finding their way and finding their prey! They don't use their eyes, though; they use their ears!

As they fly, bats make high-pitched squeaks. The sound of these squeaks travels through the air. When the sound hits an object, even a tiny one like an insect, it bounces, or echoes, back to the bat. This method of locating objects is called **sonar.**

By listening to the echoes, the bat can often tell where its meal is. Then it's just a matter of flying over and catching it. It's also a great way to avoid crashing into things like trees, houses, and even people!

Mosquito dead ahead!

THE LITTLE BROWN BAT can eat up to 1,200 flying insects in just one hour.

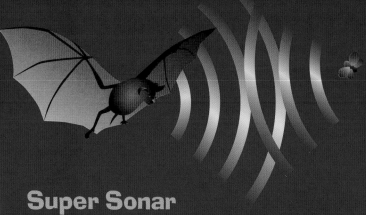

Super Sonar

Here's how sonar helps a bat find its lunch.

1. The bat squeaks. Sound waves pass through the air, moving away from the bat.

2. Sound waves strike an object, such as an insect.

3. Sound waves bounce off the object and travel back to the bat. Sound waves return faster from objects that are closer. Sound waves that bounce off more distant objects take longer to return.

Q: Why did the vampire bat get mad?

A: *He had a bat temper.*

There are all kinds of tricks to staying alive!

FACT FILE

The cuttlefish hides from predators by darkening the water with an ink substance. Ancient people used this inky brown stuff, called sepia, to make writing ink.

Here comes Mr. Dark Cloud!

Maybe I'll change to blue. . . .

Frequently changing its color helps a chameleon hide. What makes it change? Temperature, light, and even its health can cause a switch in color!

The wood frog's body freezes almost solid in winter. But it survives due to natural antifreeze called glucose, which fills its heart and lungs. This keeps the organs from freezing.

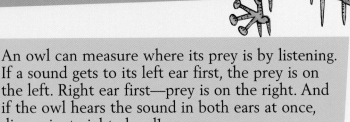

I can't wait to thaw!

An owl can measure where its prey is by listening. If a sound gets to its left ear first, the prey is on the left. Right ear first—prey is on the right. And if the owl hears the sound in both ears at once, dinner is straight ahead!

GLOSSARY

brood parasite a bird or insect that leaves its eggs in the nest of other birds or insects to be cared for

camouflage the disguise of animals or people that helps them blend in with a background

countershading a protective pattern of coloring on certain animals in which their bodies are a combination of dark and light colors

environment the surrounding area and natural conditions in which people or animals live

identical looking exactly the same

pits two small heat-sensing spots between each eye and nostril of some snakes

predators animals that hunt other animals for food

prey an animal that is hunted by another animal

pupils the openings in the centers of eyes that let in light

raptor a bird of prey, such as a vulture

sonar a system that uses sound to tell how far away an object is

INDEX